THE CHANGING FACE OF
AUSTRALIA

Text by MARGOT RICHARDSON
Photographs by CHRIS FAIRCLOUGH

an imprint of Hodder Children's Books

Produced for Hodder Wayland by
White-Thomson Publishing Ltd
2/3 St Andrew's Place
Lewes
BN7 1UP

Editor: Anna Lee
Designer: Clare Nicholas
Design concept: Chris Halls, Mind's Eye Design
Consultants: Rosemary Wanganeen, Alison Beale and Michael Waterhouse
Proofreader: Alison Cooper

First published in Great Britain in 2003 by Hodder Wayland, an imprint of
Hodder Children's Books.

British Library Cataloguing in Publication Data
Richardson, Margot
   Changing Face of Australia
   1. Australia - Juvenile literature 2. Australia - Social life and customs - 20th
   century - Juvenile literature
   I. Title II. Lee, Anna III. Australia
ISBN 0 7502 3840 2

Printed in Hong Kong

Hodder Children's Books
A division of Hodder Headline Limited
338 Euston Road, London NW1 3BH

Acknowledgements
The publishers would like to thank
the following for their contributions
to this book: Rob Bowden – statistical
research; Nick Hawken – illustrations
on pages 6, 24, 33, 38 and 40; Peter
Bull – map on page 5. All
photographs are by Chris Fairclough
except: Australian Picture Library 34;
Eye Ubiquitous 19; Margot
Richardson 7.

Contents

Darwin: A City Rebuilt

On Christmas Eve 1974, the city of Darwin was hit by a fierce tropical storm now famously known as Cyclone Tracey. During the night, the winds reached speeds of more than 215 km per hour. Terrified residents huddled in their houses as the winds screamed around them, roofs were ripped off and buildings flattened.

By dawn, 50 to 60 per cent of Darwin's buildings had been either destroyed or damaged beyond repair. Sixty-six people had been killed and thousands fled the city: the population tumbled from 47,000 to 11,000 people.

Nearly thirty years on, Darwin, the capital of Australia's Northern Territory (in the central north of the country), has been rebuilt. It is now Australia's fastest-growing capital city, with a population of nearly 69,000, thriving trade links and a well-developed tourist industry. Due to the vast size of the Australian continent, Darwin is closer to Indonesia, the Philippines and New Guinea than it is to Australia's national capital, Canberra. This means that many of Australia's exports leave the country from Darwin. A number of these exports are produced or sourced in northern Australia, including live cattle, minerals and tropical fruit.

Although freight leaves Darwin by sea, the only other route out of Darwin is a single road that heads south. However, the new AustralAsia Railway, due to be completed in 2004, will link the end of the present railway at Alice Springs, a town 1,400 km to the south, to the port at Darwin. As a result, Darwin's importance as a major trade centre linking northern Australia with South-east Asia will be increased.

▲ New buildings in Darwin are built to withstand future cyclones, and to make the most of the local climate: verandahs catch cooling breezes and provide shade from the sun.

▼ Tourists shopping in central Darwin. The city's tropical climate and laid-back atmosphere make it popular with both international and Australian tourists.

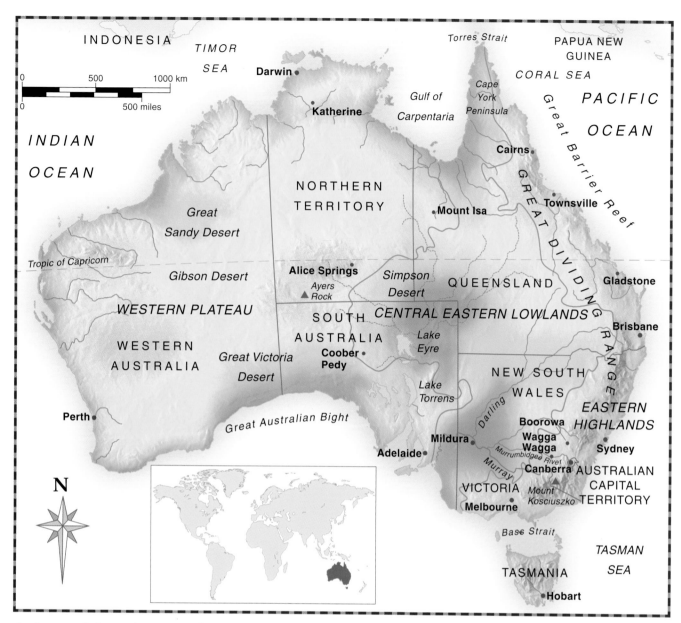

INDONESIA

TIMOR
SEA

Torres Strait

PAPUA NEW
GUINEA

CORAL SEA

PACIFIC
OCEAN

Darwin

Katherine

Gulf of
Carpentaria

Cape
York
Peninsula

Great Barrier Reef

INDIAN
OCEAN

Cairns

NORTHERN
TERRITORY

Mount Isa

Townsville

Great
Sandy Desert

Tropic of Capricorn

Gibson Desert

Alice Springs

Ayers
Rock

Simpson
Desert

QUEENSLAND

Gladstone

WESTERN PLATEAU

SOUTH
AUSTRALIA

CENTRAL EASTERN LOWLANDS

Brisbane

WESTERN
AUSTRALIA

Great Victoria
Desert

Coober
Pedy

Lake
Eyre

NEW SOUTH
WALES

GREAT DIVIDING RANGE

EASTERN
HIGHLANDS

Lake
Torrens

Darling

Perth

Great Australian Bight

Mildura

Adelaide

Boorowa
Wagga
Wagga

Murrumbidgee River

Murray

Canberra

Sydney

AUSTRALIAN
CAPITAL
TERRITORY

N

VICTORIA

Mount
Kosciuszko

Melbourne

Bass Strait

TASMAN
SEA

TASMANIA

Hobart

▲ A map of the main geographical features of Australia and places mentioned in this book.

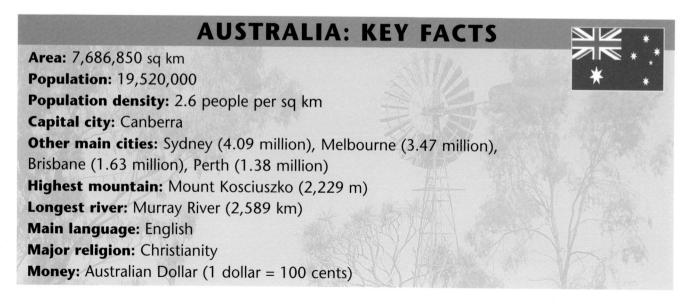

AUSTRALIA: KEY FACTS

Area: 7,686,850 sq km

Population: 19,520,000

Population density: 2.6 people per sq km

Capital city: Canberra

Other main cities: Sydney (4.09 million), Melbourne (3.47 million), Brisbane (1.63 million), Perth (1.38 million)

Highest mountain: Mount Kosciuszko (2,229 m)

Longest river: Murray River (2,589 km)

Main language: English

Major religion: Christianity

Money: Australian Dollar (1 dollar = 100 cents)

Past Times

The first Australians, the Aborigines and Torres Strait Islanders, probably arrived in what is now called Australia about 50,000 years ago. They were the only human inhabitants of the region until 1788, when a group of British prisoners and their guards arrived on the coast of present-day New South Wales (NSW). In the following years, more Europeans arrived and settled in other parts of the country.

Since then, Australia has progressed from a country dependent on agriculture to a developed nation with a variety of industries, including tourism, mining and manufacturing. Unfortunately, this process has caused immeasurable suffering to the Aboriginal people. On their arrival, the British took over the land on the principle of *terra nullius* – that the land belonged to no one – and viewed the Aborigines as scarcely human. Many of them were abused and killed, and it is only in recent years that the rights of Indigenous people have been recognized in Australian society; for example, by acknowledging their claim to land they originally occupied.

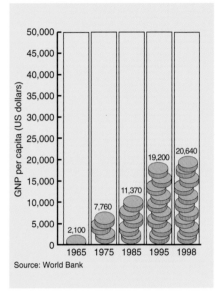

▲ *Australia's Gross National Product increased almost tenfold between 1965 and 1998.*

◄ *Many old Australian buildings are carefully preserved. This mill in Western Australia is now a tourist information centre.*

Despite its Indigenous population, up until the 1960s Australia had always regarded itself as a 'white' country. However, the arrival of immigrants from all over the world (see page 26) saw major changes in Australia's population and culture. Today, Australia's international relations, food, arts and politics are all influenced by its multicultural population.

Although Australia has democratically elected national, state and local governments, it remains a member of the British Commonwealth, with Queen Elizabeth II as the head of state. During the 1980s and 1990s many Australians felt that this arrangement was out-dated and that Australia should become an independent republic. A referendum on the issue was held in 1999, but 55 per cent of the population voted against the change.

▲ *The vast majority of Australians live in the coastal cities. The central business district of Sydney is built on the site where the British first settled in 1788.*

IN THEIR OWN WORDS

'My name is Ken Lindop. I live in Sydney and I was born in 1939. Here I am with Oscar, who's four. So much has changed since I was that age. When I was growing up we were like little British kids, even though my mother was third-generation Australian. We had a British king, read British comics and ate British food: always plain meat and boiled veg – ugh! The place where I grew up was quite rural. People bought a block of land, and sometimes whole families lived in a shed for years before they could afford to build a house. There was no way I even thought of going to university.

'Now most people are much wealthier. My three daughters all have university degrees and own their own homes. We cook Asian, Indian and Italian food all the time. I often yearn for the past, but the present is pretty good too!'

3 Landscape and Climate

Although Australia is an island it is usually called a continent, because of its vast size. It is the world's smallest continent, but is also the sixth-largest country. It consists of the mainland and the island of Tasmania to the south-east, as well as various smaller islands.

Australia can be divided into three major land regions: the Eastern Highlands, the central Eastern Lowlands and the Western Plateau.

Highlands and mountains

The fertile Eastern Highlands area consists of a narrow coastal strip and a range of mountains and plateaux called the Great Dividing Range. This runs from Cape York in the far north to southern Tasmania. Australia's highest mountains can be found in the Australian Alps.

▲ *Australia does not have land boundaries with any other country. Its border consists of 25,760 km of coastline, with many sandy beaches, such as Bondi in Sydney.*

◄ *The native vegetation of the Eastern Highlands consists of thick trees, especially eucalypts, and dense undergrowth.*

Plains

Just west of the Great Dividing Range are the Central Eastern Lowlands, a flat region stretching from the Gulf of Carpentaria in the north to Western Victoria in the south and to the centre of Australia in the west. Vegetation ranges from dense tree cover in the east to low desert bushes in the west. This region is home to Australia's largest lake, Lake Eyre, which stays dry for years and seldom fills with water.

▲ *Crops such as wheat are grown in the southern third of the central plains.*

Deserts

The Western Plateau covers almost 66 per cent of Australia's land area. It contains the country's four main deserts and some low mountain ranges. It is also hot, and mostly dry except in the far north and south-west. Much of the land is bare, with only occasional grasses and dry, spindly bushes.

IN THEIR OWN WORDS

'I'm Rebecca and I live in Coober Pedy, which is located in the Far North region of the state of South Australia. Coober Pedy is famous for mining opals, which are multi-coloured gemstones. The land affects our every move here. We're surrounded by the desert. Everything's very hot, dry and dusty. In the summer it can get up to 48 °C. We're a long way from anywhere. The nearest major city is Adelaide, which is about 850 km away. We can be considered isolated, but we now have daily air flights, bus services and private vehicle charters connecting Coober Pedy to Adelaide and Alice Springs. We have communications through satellite TV, computers, the Internet and email. The people who live in Coober Pedy love the lifestyle and the region. It's a great community town.'

A climate of extremes

The southern two-thirds of Australia has warm dry summers and cool wet winters. For example, in Melbourne the average temperature in summer is about 20 °C and in winter it is 12 °C. Snow falls in Tasmania and the Australian Alps. The northern third of Australia lies in the tropics, so temperatures are in the mid to high twenties (degrees Centigrade) all year round. It has only two seasons: wet and dry. The wet season brings heavy downpours and violent storms, including cyclones.

▲ *Many rivers in central Australia are dry for part of the year and fill with water only during the rainy season.*

Climate variability

The climate in Australia is often unpredictable, with droughts in some years and floods in others. In the 1970s scientists realized that this was due to a relationship between the ocean and the atmosphere that causes climate changes on either side of the Pacific Ocean.

The best-known change is called El Niño, when northern and eastern Australia experience droughts. The opposite is known as La Niña, which is when the same regions have widespread rain and flooding. On average, El Niño occurs every three to eight years.

Climate change

In common with the rest of the world, Australians are concerned about global warming or the 'greenhouse effect'.

◄ *Australians and tourists alike enjoy the country's mild climate. However, if temperatures rise wildlife and people will undoubtedly suffer.*

It is estimated that, in Australia, the average temperature could increase by between 0.4 and 2.0 °C by 2030, and between 1.0 and 6.0 °C by 2070. This may have far-reaching effects on the natural habitat and on farming.

Bushfires

Fires in the native vegetation (the 'bush') are sometimes started naturally by lightning strikes. But in recent times, bushfires started by careless people, or even lit deliberately, have threatened people's houses and lives. In 2001, bushfires in New South Wales and the Australian Capital Territory destroyed 150 homes and covered more than 250,000 hectares.

▲ *This woman is using a branch to beat out a small bushfire in the Northern Territory. Bushfires usually occur in summer, when the vegetation burns easily and the fires are fanned by hot, dry winds.*

IN THEIR OWN WORDS

'My name is Pat Modde and I live in Arcadia, near Sydney. I'm the captain of the Arcadia Rural Fire Brigade, which has 35 voluntary members. That's me on the left with Rob, one of our members, on the right. Arcadia is bound by true Australian bush. In winter we spend a lot of time carrying out controlled burns of the litter on the forest floor. This is to decrease the fires' intensity when they do occur.

'During the 2000-2001 fires, we were out from Christmas Day until 8th January. At first we went south of Sydney, but when it looked like our area might go up in flames we came back. Luckily, the fire never crossed the river. Then we were sent to a serious fire nearby where Elvis (the helicrane) dumped water on threatened houses. After it was all over, the city put on a huge parade for us.'

4

Natural Resources

Minerals

Australia contains deposits of almost all known minerals and the minerals industry is the nation's largest export earner: 35 per cent of all exports in 1998-99. Over the last fifty years, the country has developed into one of the world's leading miners of bauxite, diamonds, gold, iron ore, lead, manganese ore, nickel, titanium, zinc and zircon, as well as silver, copper and uranium. (Australia has one of the world's largest resources of uranium, but does not use it to generate nuclear power within the country; most of it is exported.) Because of its vast size, Australia is still under-explored, and many mineral deposits may not yet have been discovered.

Energy sources

Australia has huge resources of energy in the form of fossil fuels. Petroleum was first discovered in large quantities in the 1960s and now provides well over 50 per cent of Australia's energy needs. This is expected to rise to 60 per cent by 2010. Australia also has access to huge fields of natural gas and use

▲ *The largest bauxite smelter in Australia is located at Gladstone in Queensland. Bauxite is the ore from which aluminium is extracted.*

of gas is forecast to double within ten years. In addition, Australia is one of the top six countries in the world for reserves of black and brown coal, and is the world's largest exporter of black coal.

Solar energy

Like natural gas, the use of solar energy as an energy source for households is increasing. Household use of solar energy in 1995-96 was more than thirty times the amount used in 1974-75. While this increase seems very large, solar energy provided only 1 per cent of total household energy consumed in 1995-96.

▲ *Australia has plenty of sunshine, so solar energy is a viable alternative to other energy sources. These collecting panels, near Coober Pedy in South Australia, provide power for a telephone link.*

IN THEIR OWN WORDS

'My name is Sarah Watts and I work as a mining engineer at Mount Isa Mines in Queensland. At Mount Isa there are mines for lead/zinc/silver (these minerals are mined together) and copper.'

'The mining industry has changed a lot in recent years. There is much more mechanization and many more environmental regulations. Mount Isa was founded to service the mines. These days, mining companies rarely build new towns to service mines. 'Fly-in, fly-out' mines are much more common, where employees live in camps at the mine site for, say, two weeks, and are flown back to a base city for time off – say, one week.

'Not many women do my job, but the number of female mining engineers is increasing all the time. I have been here for four years, and my husband works here as well.'

Water

Compared to other continents, the amount of rainfall that can be used by people, animals or plants in Australia is very small. This is due to the fact that stream flow can be unpredictable, evaporation is high, and there is a lack of water storage sites. This scarcity of water has led to extensive programmes to control water supply by construction of dams, reservoirs and large tanks.

Australia has a good supply of underground water: it can be found underneath 60 per cent of the land. Some of it is too salty to use, but about 70 per cent of it can be drunk or used for irrigation. Using this water, though, has caused environmental problems by destroying the soil and reducing the water quality (see pages 20-21).

Some crops (such as fruit, vegetables and sugar cane) are dependent on irrigation or high coastal rainfall. About 3 per cent of agriculturally developed land in Australia is irrigated, most of which is found in the Murray-Darling Basin in south-west New South Wales.

▼ *Underground water is reached by drilling a bore hole. A pump, driven by a small windmill, brings water to the surface. It flows into a trough for livestock to drink, and some may be stored in a small tank for times when the wind drops.*

IN THEIR OWN WORDS

'My name is Stephen Hewitt. I run a 1,000 hectare sheep farm near Boorowa, in central New South Wales. Our sheep are Australian merinos, which produce the finest wool in the world. In the 1950s, wool was so important that Australia was said to "ride on the sheep's back". But that's long gone. In the last ten years our income from wool has really gone down. Lots of people round here got rid of their sheep and went into cattle and crops instead.

'Farming's really changed in the last twenty years or so. Now there's much more emphasis on conservation, tree planting and care of the environment. The use of pesticides and herbicides is a third of what it was – even ten years ago.'

Agriculture

Although Australia covers a vast area, due to water shortages crops can be grown on only 6 per cent of the land, while a further 58 per cent is suitable for grazing animals. The other 36 per cent is too dry to be used for farming at all.

Australian farms produce a wide variety of products: wheat, barley, oats, rice, beef cattle, sheep for meat and wool, chicken and eggs, dairy products, sugar cane, fruit and vegetables, cotton and grapes. In the past, wool was one of the most important products. Recently, crops such as cotton and grapes for wine-making have increased greatly in value.

▶ *A mixed farm in central New South Wales. The flat land in the foreground is used for growing crops and making hay, but the rocky hill is only suitable for grazing.*

Forests

Australian native forests and tree plantations provide a wide variety of resources for people, from leisure activities to wood products, such as sawn timber, fibreboard, plywood and paper. They are also a source of biological diversity and land for catching water. Australia has 16 per cent (26 million hectares) of its native forests set aside in conservation reserves. (The world average is 8 per cent.)

Fishing

Being surrounded by sea, commercial fishing is an important industry in Australia. It is the country's fourth most valuable food-producing industry – after beef, wheat and milk. Species of fish and seafood found in Australian oceans include tuna, prawns and whiting. Aquaculture, or 'fish farming', where sea creatures are raised in cages in the sea, is one of Australia's fastest-growing industries. Its value increased by more than 15 per cent each year between 1989-90 and 1998-99. The main products farmed were oysters, salmon, prawns and tuna.

▲ *Many Australians are alarmed about the rate of logging in native forests because of its impact on animals and plants. This forest is in coastal Queensland.*

IN THEIR OWN WORDS

'My name is Kevin Ingram. I come from Gladstone, in Queensland, and at the moment I'm working on a fishing boat out of Darwin. We fish for prawns and stay out at sea for up to six days at a time. We clean, cook, pack and freeze the prawns on the boat. Then they're transported by truck to all parts of the country. Lots are exported to Japan and Asia, and some goes to the Middle East.

'When my father fished in these waters they just went fishing. Now we have restrictions on our catches. We need to protect our deep-sea fish stocks, but Taiwanese and Japanese boats work just off our coasts and seem to take what they like. There are not enough fishery protection vessels and the Australian coast is too big to patrol properly.'

Native flora and fauna

Australian plants and animals are very different from those of other continents. Because the land mass was isolated from the rest of the world for a very long time, many species evolved that are not found elsewhere, or which are uncommon. Examples include marsupials such as the kangaroo; monotremes such as the platypus, and eucalyptus trees. There is also huge biodiversity: for example, there are 54,000 known species of insects, but scientists believe that at least the same number have not yet been discovered. Australian coastal waters are some of the most species-rich and diverse areas on earth.

▼ About 95 per cent of Australian mammals are unique to Australia. The koala is a marsupial that feeds on only a few types of eucalyptus leaf.

5

The Changing Environment

Flora and fauna

Since the arrival of Europeans in the eighteenth century, thousands of new plant and animal species have been introduced to Australia, and much of the native vegetation has been replaced by crops and pastures. Eighteen species of mammals have become extinct. (One example is the thylacine, or Tasmanian tiger, a stripey dog-like marsupial.) This is half of all the mammal species in the world that have become extinct in recorded history. A similar fate has affected a hundred species of plants. At present, about forty species of mammals and many hundreds of species of plants are threatened with extinction.

The Great Barrier Reef

A huge coral reef, one of the most unusual natural habitats in the world, is found off the north-east coast of Australia. Coral reefs are made by vast numbers of small marine animals grouped together,

▲ *When native woodland like this is cleared for farming, many species of animals and insects lose their home.*

IN THEIR OWN WORDS

'I'm Richard Fitzpatrick and I live in Townsville, in northern Queensland. I work as a marine photographer and film-maker specializing in sharks. This picture was taken when we were filming in a small pool.

'I'm worried about the state of the Great Barrier Reef. Water run-off from the land carrying nutrients and pollutants from farms and towns are choking and killing off the reef. We need to protect it, or it will be ruined for ever. Some parts of the reef have already been so badly damaged that they may never recover.'

all producing a hard stony material like an external skeleton. Stretching for 2,300 km, the Great Barrier Reef is the largest structure in the world made by living organisms and is probably at least 2 million years old.

People first became concerned about damage to the reef in the 1960s and the Great Barrier Reef Marine Park was declared in 1975. This was set up to ensure protection from threats such as mining, drilling for oil, commercial fishing and the tourist industry.

However, conservationists are concerned that only a small proportion of the reef is totally protected. Climate change is particularly worrying as the live coral cannot survive if the sea-water temperature rises. According to the WWF, at the current rate of warming, many of the world's coral reefs could be dead in 40 years time.

▲ *Due to the unique combination of its biological diversity and size, the reef was placed on the UNESCO World Heritage List in 1981. It is home to a huge variety of species including 1,500 of fish, 300 of corals, more than 4,000 of molluscs, over 400 of sponges, six species of turtle, the dugong, and more than 240 species of birds.*

Land damage

Since European settlement, much of Australia's deep-rooted native vegetation has been replaced by shallow-rooted crops and pastures. Although there has been less land clearing over the last thirty years, at the same time there have been increases in serious soil damage due to agriculture, irrigation, building and industry. Problems include salinization, acidification, erosion of topsoil and chemical contamination.

◀ Soil erosion has long been a problem where native vegetation has been removed. Here, much of the topsoil has been eroded and washed into the nearby Murrumbidgee River in New South Wales.

Salinity

Vast stores of salt have been buried in the Australian landscape since prehistoric times. Human activity has caused changes to the way water moves through the landscape and this can bring hidden salts to the surface. The salts concentrate in soils and rivers, and can reach levels that are toxic to plants, animals and people. Salinity can also threaten buildings, roads and power generation.

This process in soil without irrigation is called dryland salinity. About 0.6 per cent of agricultural land is affected, but this could rise to 3.6 per cent by 2050. Soil salinization is estimated to be costing the government and farming over $A100 million a year. Its cure requires massive replanting and careful management of the water table.

Water

Water salinity has become a problem in many agricultural areas, especially the Western Australia grain belt and the Murray-Darling Basin. As the ground-water levels have risen salts have seeped into the river systems. In 100 years time, some rivers may be so salty that their water is undrinkable. When this water is used for irrigation, salinization of the soil is increased.

Water quality in Australia is also threatened by the steady growth in population, urbanization and the use of catchments for recreational and commercial purposes.

▲ *An irrigation ditch in Queensland bringing water to sugar cane. If saline water is used in this way, the salt content can make the soil unusable.*

IN THEIR OWN WORDS

'My name is Geoffrey Beale. I live in south-western New South Wales, in the town of Wagga Wagga. I work as an environmental scientist, giving technical advice on salinity in soils and river systems. In this photo I'm holding a meter that can measure the salinity of water.

'At the moment my team is trying to work out how salinity will change in the future. I'm also involved in checking current salinity in the rivers and making predictions about the health of the rivers. This information helps the government and communities to plan what to do about it. Scientists and farmers have only become aware of salinity since the late 1980s and it's a big issue for farming and the environment. Now we understand it better, though, there's no reason why we can't manage it in the future.'

Air pollution

Fossil fuels – which generate greenhouse gas emissions and air pollution – provide around 90 per cent of Australia's energy needs, a higher proportion than for most other countries or regions. Because most of the population is concentrated in the coastal cities, air pollution is mainly an urban problem. It is caused by emissions from road vehicles but this is decreasing due to new technology such as unleaded petrol and catalytic converters. Moving power stations away from cities has also helped to diffuse the problem.

◀ *Constructing power stations away from cities has helped to keep the air clean in densely populated areas.*

Energy

The amount of energy used in Australia has increased over the last twenty years, and may continue to increase in the future. For example, between 1974-75 and 1995-96 household energy use increased by 46 per cent, and it is projected to increase a further 14 per cent by 2009-10. Australia's dependency on fossil fuels means that the impact of energy use is far-reaching. However, drilling for oil and mining processes are now governed by strict environmental controls.

IN THEIR OWN WORDS

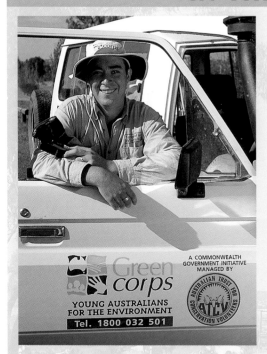

'I'm Dominic Burton and I'm a volunteer with the Green Corps. This is a force of people, aged 17 to 20, who work on practical conservation projects. We're paid an allowance, receive training, learn new skills – and enjoy the outdoors.

'In this project we're working on tree clearing and planting. There are lots of willow trees along the river bank. They slow down the water and can lead to flooding. Willows aren't native to Australia. In our parents' time they just planted anything they thought looked good, but plants like these have spread too fast. We need to get rid of them and plant more native species instead. Awareness of our environment is getting very strong in Australia, and kids are taught about it in school from an early age.'

Waste and recycling

Australia is the second-highest generator of waste per person in the world, after the USA. Until recently, much of this was buried in landfill sites, but in 1990 the Australian and New Zealand Environment Conservation Council set a goal: to reduce the amount of waste put in landfill by 50 per cent of 1990 levels by the year 2000. Now, most Australians have access to recycling schemes.

Many local councils run kerbside recycling schemes, where domestic materials are collected separately from other household waste. However, it normally costs the councils more to collect and sort the materials than they can sell them for. Even so, in order to meet waste reduction targets in the future, it will probably be necessary to collect and recycle organic materials, construction materials, electronic scrap, food and hazardous wastes.

▼ As well as recycling household rubbish such as paper, cans, glass and plastics, gas cylinders and car tyres are collected at a local rubbish dump in Queensland.

6 | The Changing Population

In 2001, Australia had an estimated population of about 19.3 million people. This population is growing at the rate of about 1.26 per cent per year, but not all this growth comes from new births. In fact, the birth rate has dropped from 3.5 children per woman in 1960 to 1.76 children per woman in 1999. In 1999-2000, 45 per cent of Australia's population growth came from overseas migration.

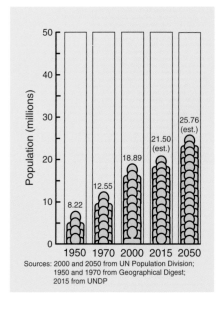

▲ *Australia's population has increased rapidly since 1950 and this growth is expected to continue.*

Ageing Australia

Like that of many Western countries, Australia's population is growing steadily older each year. This is because Australians are having fewer children, later in life, and are living longer. The average age of the population in 2001 was 35.5 years, but it is estimated that by the year 2051 the average age will be 44.1 years. Generally life expectancy is improving: the death rate in 1999 was 23 per cent lower than it was in 1989.

Elderly people tend to need more health care than younger people and, in later life, some need help in their daily lives. With a smaller proportion of young people in the population working and paying taxes, having an older population puts a strain on both society and the economy.

◄ *There are slightly more women than men in the Australian population. This is because the population is generally older, and women tend to live longer than men.*

Distribution and density

The majority of Australians live in the fertile southern and eastern coastal belt and in a smaller area in south-western Western Australia. The concentration of people in these areas did not change very much during the twentieth century, but Australians are now generally living closer to each other and in bigger urban centres. In 1906, there was about 2 sq km of land per person. By 1996, this had reduced to less than 0.5 sq km per person. Even so, Australia is still one of the most sparsely populated countries in the world.

▲ *As the number of Australians living in cities increases, more houses are needed for the population and the city grows in land area. This new housing development is on the outskirts of Perth.*

IN THEIR OWN WORDS

'My name is Jean Harris and I live in Adelaide. I grew up in a country town in South Australia. I have six children: four girls and two boys. They have so much more than I ever had in terms of material goods and expectations. My grandchildren all expect to have computers, mobile phones and stereos – before they are ten, and not even as special gifts at Christmas! We had to fight for every cent when we were young. We never borrowed money or paid for things with hire purchase. And as for credit cards – well, I just don't understand why people have so many of them and get into such trouble financially.

'I can't understand why everyone wants to live in the crowded city. It's all so noisy and I miss the big, open spaces. I'd like to live back in the country but I need my family around me and they live here.'

A nation of immigrants

At the beginning of the twentieth century, almost all Australia's inhabitants had been born in Australia, Britain and Ireland. However, by 2000, 24 per cent of the population had been born in other countries. Much of this change was due to large-scale migration after the Second World War (1939-45).

During the war, Australians had been threatened by a Japanese invasion from the north. After the war, Australians were afraid that heavily populated Asian countries might turn to Australia's vast, under-populated area. The prime minister of the time said that Australia must 'populate or perish'.

Changes in immigration

The Immigration Restriction Act of 1901, commonly known as the 'White Australia policy' was designed to keep out all Asians. Instead, after the Second World War, Australia recruited migrants from the UK and from European countries such as Italy, Greece, the Baltic countries and Yugoslavia by offering cheap fares for the long journey to Australia.

However, from the 1970s Australia started to admit more migrants from different countries, particularly people from Vietnam, China, the Philippines, Malaysia, Hong Kong and South America. By 2000, people born in Asia made up 6 per cent of Australia's population.

▼ *A variety of people of different races is now a common sight in Australia's big cities such as Sydney.*

Illegal immigrants and refugees

In recent decades, many immigrants have arrived in Australia without permission, usually in boats from South-east Asia. Since 1989, the number of immigrants and refugees arriving illegally in Australia has increased: from less than 300 in 1989-90 to nearly 7,900 between 1999 and 2001. They include Chinese, Turks, Iraqis, Pakistanis and Afghans. Almost all of them are placed in detention while the authorities decide if they are genuine refugees.

A multicultural society

Australia now has a stable society with inhabitants from all over the world. In 1996, 15 per cent of Australia's population spoke a language other than English at home. The most commonly spoken languages were Italian, Greek, Cantonese, Arabic and Vietnamese, although more than 155 other languages were also used.

▲ *An Indonesian woman with her child in Darwin. Indonesia is one of Darwin's nearest neighbours and many Indonesians who migrate to Australia make their home in the Northern Territory.*

IN THEIR OWN WORDS

'My name is Joanna and I'm 22. Both my father's parents migrated to Australia from China – my grandfather in the late 1930s and my grandmother in 1945. I haven't experienced as much racism as they have, partly because I look much less Asian, and I "blend in" more with an Anglo-Australian crowd. Also, I think Australia has become a much more accepting and multicultural society since my grandparents were young. However, if Australia is to become a truly successful multicultural society, we need to become more compassionate and generous by sharing this "lucky country" with other people from the global community, particularly those who need refuge. We also have to acknowledge the struggles of the Indigenous peoples of Australia, who should be given much more compassion and support.'

The Indigenous population

Australia's current population includes approximately 390,000 Indigenous people: the Aborigines and Torres Strait Islanders. In the early years of the country, many of these people were murdered by the white settlers – maybe as many as 50,000 over 150 years. This situation continued until 1928 when, for the first time, it was decided that such killings were unlawful.

The 'stolen generation'

In the 1930s, government officials decided that Aboriginal people should be absorbed into white society. One way to achieve this was to forcibly remove part-Aboriginal children from their parents and bring them up in institutions, where they often suffered cruelty and abuse. Some Aboriginal groups estimate that 50,000 children may have been treated in this way. The practice lasted until the 1960s and the people concerned are now known as 'the stolen generation'.

Surprisingly, few urban Australians were aware of this, mainly because it took place in inland Australia. When information about the stolen generation emerged in the 1990s, most non-Indigenous Australians were shocked to learn the extent of this history.

Aboriginal land rights

In the mid-1970s, the right to large areas of land in the Northern Territory and some of the States was granted to its Aboriginal owners. However, they could claim only land that no one else owned or leased – usually desert country.

It was not until 1992 that the High Court of Australia formally rejected the idea of *terra nullius* and the myth that Australia

▼ *Most Indigenous people still live in central and northern Australia, sometimes in remote settlements that are owned and run by their communities.*

had been unoccupied before the arrival of Europeans. This judgement is known as the Mabo decision, named after Eddie Mabo and five Torres Strait Islanders who claimed ownership of Murray Island, off the tip of Cape York. At the time, it was seen as an opportunity for reconciliation between Indigenous and non Indigenous Australians. However, many Australians still feel there is much to be done to redress past injustices experienced by Aboriginal people.

▲ *In 1972, a group of Aboriginal people set up an 'embassy' in Canberra, to attract attention to issues such as land rights. It now contains an exhibition of documents, photographs and artwork.*

IN THEIR OWN WORDS

'My name is Kevin Hill. I am an Aboriginal Heritage Officer at Yanchep National Park in Perth, Australia. I am married to a non-Aboriginal woman and we have six children and six grandchildren.

'Growing up as an Aboriginal was hard and full of challenges, especially being bullied and ignored by teachers and other students, although I had a very loving family. Later in life I became a football player which, for me, broke down a lot of barriers.

'I don't think a lot has been done to address past injustices to our people. Introducing correct Aboriginal history as a compulsory part of school education is a step in the right direction, though. Joint ventures, such as Yanchep, make other Australians more aware of respecting us and our culture. Our culture is not only different; it exists on a completely different spiritual level. I hope that one day Aboriginal people can be accepted as equals with non-Aboriginal people. We need to hold on to our culture, pass it on through our peoples and never lose it.'

7

Changes at Home

Marriage

Since the early 1990s, the number of Australian couples choosing to marry has fallen, and the age at which people first marry has increased. In particular, the number of teenage marriages dropped, probably due to changing attitudes to lone parenting and the availability of contraception and abortion. In the 1990s most people did not marry until they were 26 (women) and 29 (men). Marriage rates are probably delayed by better opportunities for higher education and work for women; decreases in the affordability of houses; and the increased acceptance of relationships outside marriage.

Relationships where couples live together but do not marry are more accepted now than they were in the past: in 1982, 5 per cent of all couples lived in such relationships, which rose to 8 per cent by 1992. In 1963, 6 per cent of births were to unmarried parents, but by 1993 this had increased to 25 per cent. This sort of living arrangement is increasingly being recognized in Australia by both legal and government systems.

▲ *Fewer marriages take place in Australia now than at any time since the 1930s. More people are opting to live together without going through a formal marriage ceremony.*

IN THEIR OWN WORDS

'I'm Rachel and I live with my mother, stepfather and four-year-old half-brother. My grandparents recently emigrated from England and have bought a house just up the road. We are a close family.

'All my closest friends live with both their natural parents, but I have met people who have step-parents or children. Whereas a family was once thought of as two parents, maybe grandparents, and lots of children, now a single mother or father and one child is accepted as a family. Perhaps the higher divorce rate has meant that we have simply developed strategies for coping with it better.'

Divorce and family breakdown

Australia's divorce rate has increased noticeably since the mid-1970s. In 1991, the Australian Institute of Family Studies found that over a thirty-year period, 40 per cent of all marriages end in divorce. However, not all family breakdowns are made official. Some married couples only separate, and unmarried relationships or splits are not registered, so the actual rate may be higher than this. These changes mean that children are growing up in a wider variety of family structures than ever before.

▼ *The majority of Australian children live with both their natural parents.*

Health

The Australian government claims that the health of Australians 'is among the best in the world'. With good-quality food, climate and housing available to most people this is not surprising. The country's health care system is based on government health insurance, called Medicare, which is financed mainly by a tax levy. This system pays for 75-85 per cent of the costs of medical and hospital care. Medical insurance is also available through private companies.

The leading causes of ill-health and death in Australia are cancer (27 per cent), heart disease (22 per cent), followed by respiratory diseases, accidents and diabetes.

Skin cancer

Australians have the highest rate of skin cancer in the world: half of all Australians will have some form of it in their lifetime, and a thousand people die from it each year.

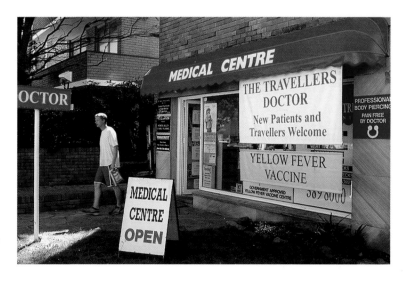

▲ A 'walk-in' medical centre in Bondi, Sydney. Such facilities are becoming increasingly popular due to the high numbers of foreign tourists now visiting Australia.

IN THEIR OWN WORDS

'My name is Andrew Marsden and I'm a doctor. I used to be in the navy, but now I specialize in health and accident prevention in industry. I fly to mines in remote areas of Western Australia and run clinics, treat injuries and help redesign machinery to prevent injuries and stress. I also work closely with the Royal Flying Doctor Service in Perth and occasionally fly with them if back-up is needed.

'These days, people are becoming more aware of their own health. Aussies tend to be a fit bunch. Many do lots of exercise – but some do too much and sports injuries are quite common! As the population grows, so does alternative medicine, especially the treatments offered by Chinese-based medicine.'

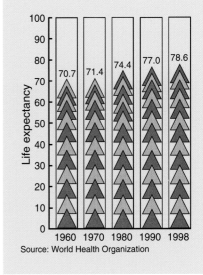

◀ *High rates of skin cancer are due to a predominantly white population and traditional outdoor lifestyle. Protective clothing is a must for the beach: most children now wear tops and hats while they play in the sun.*

Since 1985 there has been a massive campaign to teach people about the risks of exposure to the sun, and skin cancer now seems to be decreasing among people under 50 years old.

Indigenous welfare

Unfortunately, in contrast to the rest of the population, Indigenous Australians suffer from a wide range of disadvantages. Their babies are more likely to die around the time of birth, and according to a government report, published in 1999, 'Those who survive are more likely than other Australians to live in poor conditions ... to develop a range of chronic diseases, to be admitted to hospital, and to die at a young age.'

▲ *The life expectancy of most Australians has increased slowly but surely since 1960.*

Education

Education is controlled and organized by each state or territory government, so there is some variation between different areas. However, all children must go to school between the ages of six and 15 (16 in Tasmania). About three-quarters of schools are run by the governments and are free. The others are run privately, and are usually associated with religious groups.

Most children start primary school at the age of five. Before that they may have some sort of 'early years' or kindergarten education. School can then last for twelve or thirteen years, divided into six or seven years of primary and a further five or six years of secondary school. The final two years are not usually compulsory but are necessary to qualify for university and some colleges.

Students can then go on to further study at universities, colleges and institutes of Technical and Further Education (TAFE). In recent years, further education has been encouraged by the government and more students completed such courses in the 1990s than in the 1980s. It is hoped that, in the future, this will result in a more highly skilled labour force. Another feature of higher education is the increasing number of students from overseas, many of whom are from Asia.

◄ *Students at the University of Sydney. The university was established in 1850 and is the oldest in Australia.*

Religion

Officially, Australia is a Christian country, but only about 70 per cent of the population describe themselves as Christian. Of these, there are many different Christian denominations: the main ones being Catholic (27 per cent), Anglican (22 per cent), Uniting Church, Presbyterian/Reformed and Orthodox. Other religions practised in Australia are Islam (1 per cent), Buddhism (1 per cent), Judaism (0.45 per cent) and Hinduism (0.38 per cent). The numbers of Muslims and Buddhists in Australia are growing rapidly.

▶ *A Uniting church in Mildura, NSW.*

IN THEIR OWN WORDS

'My name is Glen, I'm 15 and I live in Sydney. I go to a state secondary school and I'm in year nine. School is all right. My favourite subjects are mathematics, history, woodwork and agriculture. The things I don't like about it are most of the teachers, not having the freedom to do whatever you want and the high prices in the canteen! Since my parents were young education has changed a lot. Back then they had to work a lot harder and they were hit if they were bad. Now some of my classes are really easy. If we play up all the teachers can do is yell at us and that doesn't work any more.

'When I leave school I don't want to go to university. Instead, I'll go straight to the police academy. My hope for the future is to become a detective.'

Sport

Many Australians are passionate about sport. Rugby League, cricket, tennis, Australian Rules football, swimming, sailing, horse racing and surfing are all popular. Australian Olympics teams were notable in the 1996 and 2000 Olympics for winning more medals per head of population than almost any other country in the world.

◄ *Winners line up to receive their prizes at a beach life-saving competition in Western Australia. Competitions like these, where men and women test their skills in the water, are held all over Australia.*

The arts

Australia has a vibrant arts culture that includes literature, music, dance and art of every kind. Every state has its own symphony orchestra, ballet and opera performances. There are thriving pop, rock and folk music scenes. Artists have been producing work almost since the first settlements. Aboriginal artists, musicians and performers have become both numerous and successful since the 1980s.

Films have been made in Australia since 1896 and the country's film industry gained international recognition during the 1970s. Since then, films such as *Mad Max*, *Muriel's Wedding* and *Babe* have had worldwide success. *The Matrix*, *Moulin Rouge* and *Star Wars Episode II* were all made at the Sydney Fox Studios, which opened in the 1990s.

IN THEIR OWN WORDS

'My name is Hannah MacDougall and I'm a theatre director. I work in professional theatre and also community arts, which involves people from many different walks of life in performance. Theatre in Australia has changed dramatically in recent decades. In the past, most of the theatre produced was traditional opera, ballet and plays that represented Western culture. Today, far more funding goes towards theatre that communicates about a diverse range of cultures using music, stories and costume. Youth arts, multicultural arts and Indigenous arts are now highly-respected.

'Another change in the industry is that more women work in the arts than ever before. However, good roles for actresses are still hard to come by and I'd like to see more women theatre technicians and writers.'

Food and wine

In the second half of the twentieth century, Australia's food started to become much more diverse as Australians learned about immigrants' cooking; first, that of Europe and, more recently, Asia. At the same time, Australians have become very aware of healthy eating. Low-fat foods, healthy oils and fresh produce feature much more in the Australian diet than they did twenty or thirty years ago.

Wine production has become one of Australia's fastest-growing industries since the late 1970s. Although wine has been produced in Australia almost since European settlement, since the 1970s its quality has increased so much that it now rivals and often surpasses wines made in European countries.

▲ *Australians now enjoy one of the most diverse choices of food in the world, from Italian, Greek and Lebanese to Vietnamese, Malaysian and Thai. This Italian café is in Adelaide.*

8

Changes at Work

Working patterns

Thirty or so years ago, Australians could expect to have 'a job for life' if they wished, but now jobs are becoming less secure, and unemployment is increasing – particularly for less-skilled workers.

There is an increasing trend for people to work in temporary or casual jobs, or to work part-time. In addition, more Australians are becoming self-employed (known as 'own-account' workers in Australia), although this is difficult to measure as this type of working arrangement can be hard to define. Australians are also working longer hours than ever before: in 1998 it was calculated that 27 per cent of employed people worked more than 44 hours a week, and 9 per cent worked 60 or more hours per week. This is a higher proportion than in many other countries. These changes have prompted some fears about workers' health and quality of life, both at work and at home.

▲ A shopping mall in Adelaide. Many of Australia's casual and temporary workers are employed in the retail industry.

Women at work

Since the 1950s, the number of women who are employed has nearly doubled. In the 1950s, women who married were expected to give up work and to support their husbands but since then roles for women have gradually changed to give women equal rights in education and employment. Now, of working women, 61 per cent are married and 57 per cent work in full-time jobs.

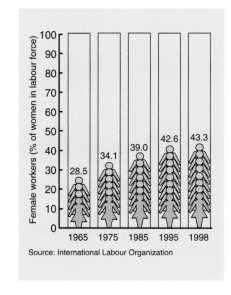

Source: International Labour Organization

▲ Since 1965 there has been a steady rise in the number of women in the Australian workforce.

The remaining 43 per cent who work part time are often students, or women with young children.

Even though more women have taken up jobs in recent years, most still work in traditionally 'female' roles, such as clerical work, sales, nursing and teaching. Men, on the other hand, dominate in trades, manufacturing and transport jobs.

▶ *A female park attendant mows the grass in Townsville, Queensland. She is the only woman doing such a job in her town; all the other park workers are men.*

IN THEIR OWN WORDS

'My name is Trish Fairley and I run a company that trains people in communication, leadership and teamwork. In my lifetime there have been enormous changes in opportunities for women in the workplace. In my mother's era a woman's main role was seen to be that of housewife. In the mid-1960s when a female government worker married she had to resign from her job.

'Since then, conditions, pay and opportunities have improved enormously and women now have the same legal rights as men. However, the "glass ceiling", the invisible barrier stopping women reaching top levels in business, is still firmly in place. Women who have family responsibilities find it difficult to meet the expectations of organizations that demand long work hours, inflexible meeting times (e.g. early mornings) and full-time employment. I hope that in future companies will encourage all employees to have a healthier balance between their private life and their work.'

Changes in farming

As in most developed countries, Australia's farms have changed dramatically in just a hundred years. Farms that once employed hundreds of labourers are now operated by just a few people using modern machinery. Today, only 5 per cent of Australia's workforce are engaged in farming, which is half the number of the 1950s. Another trend is the declining importance of small farms. In 1996-97, about one-tenth of farms carried out almost half of farm business.

◀ *Rounding up cattle on horseback on a station (farm) near Katherine in the Northern Territory. Such work is increasingly carried out with motorbikes, or sometimes even helicopters.*

Changes in industry

For much of Australia's history, its economy has been dependent on production industries such as farming, mining, manufacturing and building. In the 1960s, these industries employed about 46 per cent of the workers. However, by the 1990s, this share had gone down to 28 per cent, partly due to more efficient mechanization and technology.

Instead, more people are now employed in service industries such as retailing, finance, insurance, property, health and administration. There has been a big increase in the number of these jobs in recent years: in the decade from the mid-1980s to the mid-1990s, the number of workers in service industries increased by 31 per cent, or 1.4 million jobs. These changes in industry have had a marked effect on

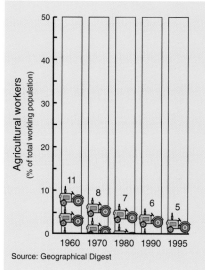

Source: Geographical Digest

▲ *The percentage of the Australian workforce employed in agriculture has decreased by more than half since 1960.*

the types of jobs available today. New technology and the increasing use of computers mean that there are more opportunities for skilled workers than there are for unskilled people such as factory workers and labourers.

In addition, there is increased competition from Asia. As Asian countries have developed economically, they have been able to compete with Australian industries, and have the advantages of lower labour costs and fewer controls on pollution.

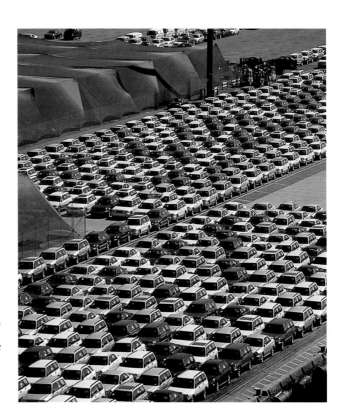

▶ *Some cars are manufactured in Australia, and many are imported from Asian countries. Some of these vehicles on a dock in Sydney are covered to protect them from the sun and damage by hailstones.*

IN THEIR OWN WORDS

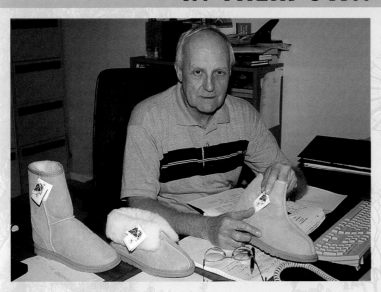

'I'm Leigh Collien and I live in Sydney. I work for a company in the leather tanning industry. For more than 30 years we have supplied machinery and spare parts to make leather. In recent years the tanning industry has declined in Australia, due to the high cost of manufacture, high wages, very strict controls on pollution and, recently, the abolition of import tariffs (taxes on the countries supplying goods to Australia) by the government.

'Our company has been finding business quite difficult, but there is still a small industry in Australia for the production of special types of leathers: kangaroo (which is very strong) and sheepskin with the wool left on. These sheepskins are made into slippers and boots – called 'Ugh Boots' in Australia. The wool is on the inside of the boots, and it keeps your feet nice and warm!'

Tourism

A 'service' industry that has grown markedly in recent years, tourism is now a major part of the Australian economy. Nearly 70 per cent of tourism income is generated by Australians going on holiday, but the number of international visitors grew during the 1990s. In 1993-94 there were 3.17 million overseas visitors. By 2001 this had grown to 4.8 million, an increase of over 50 per cent.

Tourism employs about 513,000 people, which is 6 per cent of all employed Australians. But by adding on the indirect effects of tourism (such as demand for buildings and transport), the proportion in work as a result of tourism is closer to 10 per cent. Even so, many of these are casual employees. For example, of all the people employed in accommodation, cafés and restaurants, nearly 60 per cent have casual jobs and are likely to work part-time. People who work in tourism are actively encouraged to gain nationally recognized training, either by full-time further education, or by combining study with workplace experience. An ability to speak an Asian or European language is an advantage.

▲ *Because Australia is so far from other countries, most Australians take holidays within the country. Here, a beach town in Queensland is set up to cater for visitors.*

◄ *Aboriginal art and culture have become a major tourist attraction in some parts of Australia, particularly the Northern Territory. This man makes and sells didgeridoos, a traditional Aboriginal musical instrument.*

IN THEIR OWN WORDS

I'm Jemimah and I work for Virgin Blue, a new Australian airline. I work in customer services: checking in passengers and their bags, issuing boarding passes and marshalling on the tarmac.

'Because distances are so vast in Australia, it's a long drive from one capital city to another. Virgin Blue is the country's only low-fare airline, so it gives thousands of people the chance to fly. The aviation industry is now in a period of massive growth. We have over 1,700 staff across the country and the company is still growing. I enjoy working in tourism because I get travel discounts, but also because it's fun, fast paced and no two days are ever the same.'

Unemployment

From the end of the Second World War in 1945 to the early 1970s, the rate of unemployment in Australia was low, staying below 3 per cent of the workforce. Since then, changes in unemployment have followed highs and lows of the economy, increasing at times to a maximum of 10 or 11 per cent just after periods of recession.

Unemployment among skilled people is usually lower than for unskilled. In the 1990s, it was highest among people working in sales, trades and labouring, and the lowest rates were found among managers and professionals.

▲ Both skilled and unskilled people are employed on this building site. Yet although they work in the same industry, the skilled workers are less likely to experience unemployment during their working lives.

9 The Way Ahead

In the past, Australians always considered their country to be egalitarian, a place where anyone could have 'a fair go', social class was not supposed to matter, and 'mateship' was central to the way of life. Today, many Australians are confronting the reality that some people – particularly Indigenous Australians – have not always had a 'fair go' and are working together to create a more equal society.

Throughout the nineteenth and twentieth centuries, many Australians suffered from a sense of inferiority when comparing themselves to the rest of the world. Other countries – especially the UK and USA – were often seen as being more advanced, more cultured and more powerful. People talked about suffering from a 'cultural cringe'. Europe was viewed as the centre of excellence for the arts, and Australians felt dependent on American military power.

Since the 1990s Australia has increasingly looked towards Asia due to links via trade, investment, culture, education and families. Now, though, it no longer looks to other countries for approval.

▶ *Many members of today's younger generation are determined that all Australians will have opportunities to succeed in the future.*

IN THEIR OWN WORDS

'We're Lachlan, Jacqueline and Chris and we live with our parents in Sydney. Since our mum and dad were kids, there are more people, and it's harder to buy a house or get a job.

'Since the 2000 Olympics, Australia has become much more popular. People know about us because of the Olympics, Australian movies and actors. Sometimes we get worried about problems with defence, refugees and racial gangs. Even so, we still think it's a safer and more democratic place to live than other countries.

'We really like Australia because it's got good weather, loads of beaches, lots of good food, and because everyone's looked after. We also think the Aussie sense of humour is pretty cool, too!'

Its successes in many fields – culminating in the staging of the Sydney 2000 Olympic games – have led to a new-found sense of national pride and confidence.

Australia has its own, unique share of social and environmental problems. Issues such as land degradation, rural hardship, Indigenous welfare and refugees are being tackled, although they are sometimes remote from the day-to-day lives of urban Australians. Like most Western countries, there are modern challenges such as supporting the ageing population and coping with job insecurity. However, as long as equality remains a part of Australian society, Australians can face the future with confidence.

▶ *Old and new buildings in Sydney demonstrate the rapid progress Australia has made in its recent history.*

Glossary

Biodiversity The variety of plants and animals in a particular environment.

Bush Country that is not farmed and contains native vegetation.

Catchment The land from which rainfall flows into a river, lake or dam.

Continent A large, continuous expanse of land.

Cyclone A tropical storm caused by winds rotating inwards to an area of low pressure.

El Niño Means 'the boy' or 'the Christ child' in Spanish. It is the name given to warming of the eastern Pacific Ocean off the coast of Peru, which is said to occur near Christmas.

Eucalypt A fast-growing, evergreen Australian tree.

Exports Goods or services that are sold and sent to another country.

Extinct No longer in existence.

Fossil fuels A natural fuel, such as petroleum, coal or gas found in the earth.

Freight Goods transported by truck, train or ship.

Greenhouse effect The name for a theory that increased amounts of gases in the earth's atmosphere (including carbon dioxide) have increased its ability to absorb heat energy from the sun.

Immigrants People who have left their country of birth to live permanently in a different country.

Indigenous Originating naturally in a particular place.

Institution An organization providing residential care for people.

Irrigation Water supplied to land or crops by channels or pipes.

Landfill A site where rubbish is buried.

La Niña Means 'the girl' in Spanish. It is the name for the cooling of the waters of the eastern Pacific; the opposite or reverse of the 'El Niño' effect.

Logging Cutting down a forest in order to sell the wood.

Marsupial A type of mammal whose young are born before they are fully developed and are carried in a pouch on the mother's front. Examples include kangaroos, wallabies and koalas.

Migration Moving from one place to another, usually to find work.

Monotreme A type of mammal that lays eggs and has one body opening for both excretion and reproduction. All the living species of monotremes (platypus and echidnas) are found only in Australia and New Guinea.

Ore A solid material from which a metal or valuable mineral can be extracted.

Plateau A high, flat area of land.

Population All the people who live in a particular place or country.

Recession An economic decline when trading and manufacturing are reduced.

Referendum A general vote by people on a single political question.

Republic A state that has an elected president rather than a king or queen.

Saline Containing salt.

Solar Relating to the sun or its rays.

Species A group of living organisms that are similar enough to be able to breed with each other.

Surfing Riding a surfboard on a wave towards the shore.

Tropical A wet, warm climate.

UNESCO United Nations Educational, Scientific and Cultural Organization.

Urban Built-up as in a town or city.

Wallaby An Australian marsupial, similar to but smaller than the kangaroo.

Water table The level of the ground below which it is saturated with water.

WWF A worldwide conservation organization. Formerly known as the World Wildlife Fund.

Further Information

Books

Australia by Mary V. Fox (Heinemann, 2001)

Australian Animals by Caroline Arnold (HarperCollins, 2000)

Country Fact Files: Australia by Robert Allison (Hodder Wayland, 1999)

Festivals of the World: Australia by Diana Griffiths (Gareth Stevens, 1999)

Great Barrier Reef by David Doubilet (National Geographic Society, 2002)

Lizard Island: Science and Scientists of Australia's Great Barrier Reef by Sneed B. Collard (Franklin Watts, 2000)

Next Stop Australia by Fred Martin (Heinemann, 1998)

Peoples Under Threat: Australian Aborigines by Helen L. Edmunds (Hodder Wayland, 1995)

Sydney by Christine Hatt (Belitha Press, 2001)

Videos

All available from ABC Online (http://shop2.abc.net.au/)

Australia – The Big Picture (Australian Broadcasting Corporation)

The Dreaming – Animated Aboriginal Stories From Around Australia (Aboriginal Nations Pty Ltd/Australian Broadcasting Corporation)

Nature of Australia (Australian Broadcasting Corporation)

100 years – The Australian Story (Australian Broadcasting Corporation)

Websites

http://www.aboriginalaustralia.com
Information about art and culture, including the 'Didgeridoo University of Central Australia'.

http://www.aboriginalaustralia.com
A web company with total Aboriginal ownership. Download information, talk directly with remote Aboriginal communities and buy authentic Aboriginal items.

http://www.acfonline.org.au
Australian Conservation Foundation: information on local conservation issues.

http://www.auslig.gov.au
The website of Geoscience Australia (National Mapping Division) with maps and geographical information.

http://www.foxstudios.com.au
The website of the Sydney Fox film studios.

http://www.gbrmpa.gov.au
Official website of the Great Barrier Reef Marine Park Authority.

http://www.sunsmart.com.au
Sun care and skin cancer information.

http://www.wwf.org
WWF Australia with information on environmental issues, including the Great Barrier Reef.

Useful addresses

Australian High Commission
The Strand
London WC2B 4LA
Tel: 020 7379 4334
Website: http://www.australia.org.uk

Australian Tourist Commission
Gemini House
10-18 Putney Hill
London SW15 6AA
Tel: 020 8780 2229
Website: http://www.australia.com

Index